Bridgestone
B O O K S

Native American Life

The Southwest Indians

Daily Life in the 1500s

by Mary Englar

Consultant:
Troy Rollen Johnson, PhD
American Indian Studies
California State University
Long Beach, California

Capstone
press

Mankato, Minnesota

Bridgestone Books are published by Capstone Press,
151 Good Counsel Drive, P.O. Box 669, Mankato, Minnesota 56002.
www.capstonepress.com

Library of Congress Cataloging-in-Publication Data
Englar, Mary.
    The Southwest Indians: daily life in the 1500s / by Mary Englar.
        p. cm.—(Bridgestone books. Native American life)
    Summary: "A brief introduction to Native American tribes of the Southwest, including their social
structure, homes, food, clothing, and traditions"—Provided by publisher.
    Includes bibliographical references and index.
    ISBN 0-7368-4319-1 (hardcover)
    1. Indians of North America—Southwest, New—History—16th century—Juvenile literature.
2. Indians of North America—Southwest, New—Social life and customs—16th century—Juvenile
literature. 3. Southwest, New—Antiquities—Juvenile literature. I. Title. II. Series.
E78.S7E54 2006
976.004'97—dc22   2005001651

Editorial Credits
Christine Peterson, editor; Jennifer Bergstrom, set designer; Ted Williams, book designer;
    Kelly Garvin, photo researcher/photo editor; maps.com, map illustrator

Photo Credits
American Museum of Natural History, cover
Art Resource, N.Y./Smithsonian American Art Museum, Washington, D.C., 10, 12
Courtesy of the Rockwell Museum of Western Art, Gift of Robert F. Rockwell, Jr. (detail), 20
The Granger Collection, New York, 16
North Wind Picture Archives, 6, 8, 18
Stock Montage Inc., 14

1 2 3 4 5 6 10 09 08 07 06 05

Table of Contents

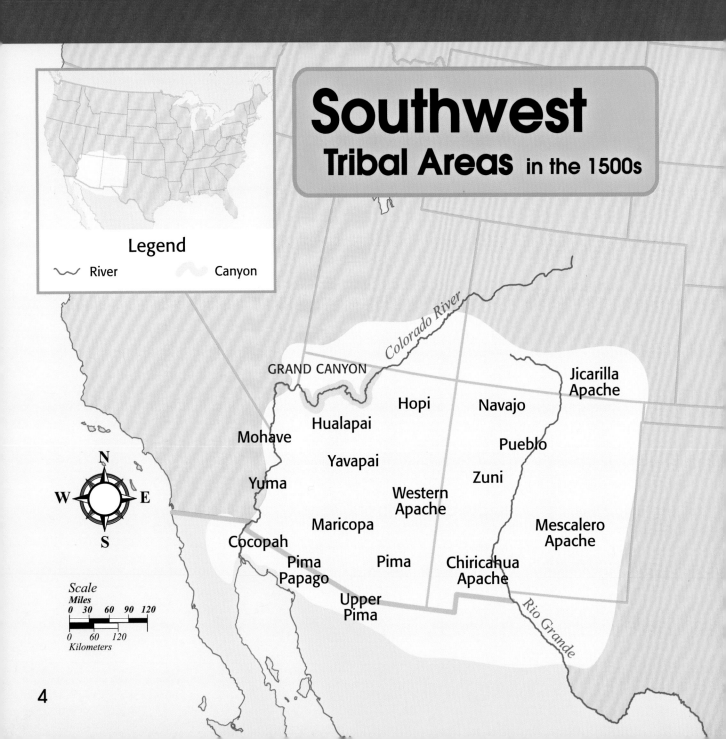

Southwest
Tribal Areas in the 1500s

Legend

~ River   ~ Canyon

N W E S

GRAND CANYON

Colorado River

Jicarilla Apache

Hopi

Navajo

Hualapai

Mohave

Pueblo

Yavapai

Zuni

Yuma

Western Apache

Maricopa

Mescalero Apache

Cocopah

Pima

Pima
Papago

Pima

Chiricahua Apache

Upper
Pima

Rio Grande

Scale
Miles
0   30   60   90   120

0   60   120
Kilometers

4

The Southwest and Its People

For at least 11,000 years, Native Americans have lived in the dry Southwest. This area includes today's U.S. states of Arizona, New Mexico, Utah, and Colorado. When European explorers arrived in the 1600s, at least 20 tribes lived in the area.

Native Americans knew the area's **plateaus** and deserts well. In the 1500s, their culture **thrived** on the land around them. Some tribes farmed. Others moved often to gather plants and to hunt. The rough, dry land shaped their daily life.

◀ Traditional tribal areas of Southwest Native Americans are shown over present-day borders.

Social Structure

Most Southwest Indians lived in family groups. The Pueblo and other tribes lived in large family groups called **clans**. Parents, grandparents, aunts, uncles, and children lived together in villages. Chiefs led most villages. Chiefs and spiritual leaders made most decisions for the village.

The Apache and the Navajo lived in family groups called **bands**. These small groups moved each season to find food. Chiefs or headmen led most bands. Apache leaders won power through battles with other tribes.

◀ In the Southwest, family groups called clans worked together to gather food and make pottery.

Homes

Southwest tribes made homes from materials they found in nature. They used dirt, trees, grasses, and animal skins to build their homes.

Some tribes built pueblos from clay or stone bricks. Tribes near rivers mixed clay, straw, and water to make **adobe** bricks. Tribes that lived on **mesas** carved stone bricks.

The Apache built wickiups or tepees. Wickiups had rounded wood frames covered with grasses. Tepees had cone-shaped frames covered with animal skins.

◄ Some Southwest tribes gathered clay from nearby rivers to make adobe bricks for their homes.

Food

In the 1500s, corn was the main food for most Southwest tribes. The Pueblo and Yuma grew corn near rivers. They used river water to **irrigate** dry land. Women ground corn into flour. They dried extra corn for winter. Winters were too dry to grow fresh food.

Finding food was often hard in the Southwest's dry **climate**. Native Americans gathered wild vegetables and berries. Many tribes collected cactus fruits. Men hunted deer and rabbits for meat.

◄ Hopi women used ground corn to make a flat bread called Piki (PEE-kee).

Clothing

Some Southwest tribes made clothing from animal skins and soft tree bark. The Apache made moccasins, shirts, and skirts from soft deerskins. In the desert, the Yuma made shoes from willow tree bark.

The Navajo and the Pueblo made clothing out of cotton and wool. These tribes grew, harvested, and spun cotton into cloth. In the late 1500s, some tribes began raising sheep. They wove sheep's wool into shirts, pants, and skirts. They made wool blankets to wear around their shoulders.

◀ Many Southwest tribes sewed colorful beads on their moccasins. These beads were often made from river clay.

14

Trading and Economy

Most Southwest tribes lived on what they gathered, grew, and hunted. Tribes traded for things they could not get in their area. The Pueblo were good farmers. They traded extra corn for buffalo hides and deerskins.

The Navajo and Apache were hunters. They brought hides of buffalo, bear, and deer to Pueblo villages. They traded for corn, seeds, and cloth.

Tribes also traded knowledge with each other. They shared skills such as farming and weaving.

◄ The Pueblo traveled across the Southwest to trade with other tribes. Mules carried blankets and other goods.

16

Leisure Time

Families spent much of their free time playing games. Guessing games were favorites. Many tribes played *patol*. Players tossed marked sticks and guessed how they would land. The Navajo played the moccasin game. One player hid a stone in one of four moccasins. The other player had to guess which shoe held the stone. The Hopi played the same game with wooden cups.

Foot races were also popular. Zuni runners raced using sticks. Runners used their toes to kick sticks ahead as they ran.

◀ Pueblo men play *patol* in 1890. This game has been played the same way for hundreds of years.

Traditions

Southwest tribes held **ceremonies** to honor nature. The Pueblo Corn Dance celebrated good harvests. Tribes thanked the earth for their food.

The Hopi and other tribes honored **kachinas**. They prayed to these spiritual beings for rain and a long life.

Some ceremonies celebrated daily life. The Apache Sunrise Ceremony honored a girl when she became a woman. The Navajo held a feast for a new baby. The first person to make the baby smile cooked a special meal.

◄ The Zuni danced in honor of kachinas during the Shalako Ceremony. They asked kachinas for rain and good crops.

Passing On Traditions

In Southwest tribes, elders taught traditions of the tribe to children. In the 1500s, most tribes did not have a written language. Elders told stories to teach children about the tribe's history and beliefs.

Tribes taught children the traditions of daily life. The Navajo showed children how to weave blankets. Pueblo women taught girls how to make pottery. Children carried on the traditions of their tribes. When children became adults, they shared their tribe's skills and beliefs with others.

◄ In the Southwest, fathers carved pictures and told stories to teach children about their tribe's past.

Glossary

adobe (uh-DOH-bee)—a building material made of clay mixed with water and straw, and dried in the sun

band (BAND)—a group of Indian people who are related to each other; a band is smaller than a tribe.

ceremony (SER-uh-moh-nee)—formal actions, words, or music performed to mark an important occasion

clan (KLAN)—a large group of related families

climate (KLYE-mit)—the usual weather in a place

irrigate (IHR-uh-gate)—to bring water to dry land or crops

kachina (kah-CHEE-nuh)—a friendly spirit or the dancer who imitates the spirit

mesa (MAY-suh)—a hill with steep sides and a flat top

plateau (pla-TOH)—area of high, flat land

thrive (THRIVE)—to do well

Read More

Bishop, Amanda, and Bobbie Kalman. *Nations of the Southwest.* Native Nations of North America. New York: Crabtree, 2003.

Gray-Kanatiiosh, Barbara A. *The Pueblo.* Native Americans. Edina, Minn.: Abdo, 2002.

Internet Sites

FactHound offers a safe, fun way to find Internet sites related to this book. All of the sites on FactHound have been researched by our staff.

Here's how:
1. Visit *www.facthound.com*
2. Type in this special code **0736843191** for age-appropriate sites. Or enter a search word related to this book for a more general search.
3. Click on the **Fetch It** button.

FactHound will fetch the best sites for you!

Index